EXPLORERS

Knights & Castles

Written by: Kirsty Neale
Illustrated by: Laszlo Veres

igloo

Mighty Castles

A castle is a strong building made to keep out enemies and attackers. In Europe, the first castles were wooden **forts**. Over time, they were replaced with much tougher stone walls.

A castle was usually owned by a rich and powerful lord, who also ruled over the surrounding towns, villages and land.

ramparts (outer walls)

arrow slit

Motte and bailey

In a motte and bailey castle, a wooden fort was built on top of a mound of earth, or motte. The flat bailey was protected by a tall wooden fence.

motte

bailey

Arrows were fired through small slits,

tower

battlements

◄ The keep was a strong tower. Inside were bedrooms, the Great Hall, a large kitchen and a prison.

▼ Castle walls were hard for an enemy to knock down. Some were up to 12 feet (3.5m) thick at the bottom.

keep

portcullis

lord

bailey (inner courtyard)

soldiers

▲ A lord kept an army of knights and soldiers to protect everyone who lived in the castle from enemy attacks.

called loopholes, in the castle walls.

1 Saumur in France was built by an English king, Henry II, to replace a castle that was destroyed in battle.

2 Castel del Monte in Italy has eight sides, and its towers are octagon-shaped, too.

Castles Around the World

Between 1000 and 1500 AD, most castles were built to keep out enemies. Later on, they were built as a way to show off a person's wealth and importance. We can still see castles all over the world.

7 Himeji-jo was one of many castles built by Japan's powerful **warlords**, who were bitter enemies.

In Japan, 'jo' means castle, and in

3 The castle of Masada was built on high, rocky cliffs in Israel almost 2,000 years ago.

4 In the 12th century, more than 2,000 knights lived at Krak des Chevaliers in Syria.

6

1

2

4

3

7

5

6 Harlech Castle is built overlooking the sea on a cliff top in Wales. It is famous for its huge gatehouse.

5 It took ten years to build the Red Fort in India. The castle is named after its red sandstone walls.

Building a Castle

Medieval castles were expensive to build. Materials were heavy and often had to be carried long distances. It could take up to ten years to build a castle.

Tools

Many medieval tools were similar to the ones we use today. Craftsmen worked with picks, mallets and chisels made from wood and iron.

stonemason's mark

square

comb chisel

mallet

pick

Stone was lifted using a **treadwheel**. As a man inside it walked, the wheel turned and lifted the stone.

Logs brought from the nearest woods were used to make a castle's wooden doors, floors and ceilings.

After 40 years of building, Caernarfon

As many as 2,000 skilled craftsmen, including stonemasons, carpenters, **quarrymen**, blacksmiths and **ditchers**, might be hired to work on one castle.

▼ Builders used scaffolding made from wooden poles and planks, and lifted their materials with **pulleys** or hoists.

treadwheel

wooden scaffolding

Inside a Castle

Many people lived inside a medieval castle, and it was also a **stronghold** where weapons were made and stored. A cook and servants prepared food for everyone in the large castle kitchen.

▶ The kitchen had a huge fireplace used for roasting meat, and a special oven for baking bread. Scullions kept the room clean.

The Great Hall was used for dining, and as a meeting room. Musicians played from the minstrels' gallery.

A lord's family slept in the **solar**. It was a comfortable room, also used for reading and embroidery.

Clothes, coins, jewels, furs and spices

Prisoners were kept, and sometimes tortured, in a **dungeon** built under the keep, or one of the towers.

Prayers were said in the **chapel** before breakfast, mid-morning, in the evening and before bed.

were stored in a room called a wardrobe.

Castle People

As well as the lord and his family, a castle was home to knights, **squires** and servants, who did all kinds of different jobs. It was a crowded, noisy and sometimes smelly place.

servant

baby bath

servant bringing logs for the fire

lady doing embroidery

▶ The lady of the castle often spent time sewing. She was also in charge of the servants, who kept the castle clean, warm and well-lit.

A gong farmer had the nasty job of

Visitors to a castle were announced by a herald, who also delivered messages for the lord.

A blacksmith made tools, weapons and horseshoes from metal. **Longbows** and **crossbows** were made by a bowyer.

◀ Carpenters were skilled craftsmen who made many important things for the castle, such as furniture, roofing and **siege engines**.

Skilled servants

Cordwainers made shoes for everybody, and gardeners grew herbs to make medicines. Surgeons sometimes had to saw off limbs if knights were injured in battle.

herbs

saw

shoe

emptying the castle latrines at night!

Food and Fun

Entertainers were an important part of castle life. Musicians, jugglers, acrobats and **jesters** performed after the evening meal and on special occasions, when feasts were held for visitors.

Squires (knights' assistants) often served at feasts. They carried food and poured water, so guests could wash their sticky fingers.

▶ **Troubadours** went from castle to castle, singing romantic songs. **Minstrels** also played as the guests ate.

▶ A jester told jokes or riddles and pulled faces. Some also juggled.

Salt was so expensive that it was only

At a feast, guests were served in the Great Hall. They ate courses of meat, such as **venison**, duck or pheasant, and fish. Sweet puddings followed.

given to lords or royalty at feasts.

A Knight's Job

▼ The earliest knights wore chain mail for protection in battle. They also carried a shield decorated with a **coat-of-arms**. This helped other knights to tell friends from enemies.

Knights were very important men. They were paid by the lord to fight and win battles. It took fourteen years to train as a knight, and boys began at seven years old.

▶ When a man became a knight, he was 'dubbed', or lightly hit, by his lord. He was also given his own sword.

From about 1400, knights wore heavy steel plates for even better protection. These were expensive to make.

In training, a young knight fought on

A knight was sometimes given a ring by the lady he loved and served, as a sign that she loved him, too.

Knights went hunting with **falcons** and hounds, catching birds and rabbits to eat.

piggyback until he could ride a horse!

Tournaments

Knights showed off their skills at a sporting event called a tournament. They competed in front of lords, ladies and other knights to see who was best at fighting and horse-handling.

▼ In a jousting, or tilting, competition, a knight tried to knock an opponent off his horse using a lance.

lance

shield with coat-of-arms

A knight could win a fortune or lose

If a lady watching the tournament was impressed with a knight, she sometimes gave him her scarf or a ring.

For jousting, a knight wore a strong, heavy tilting helmet. He peered out at his opponent through the narrow eyeslit.

crowd

tent in which a knight kept his gear

A knight put on protective gear before fighting. There were so many parts to wear that getting dressed could take an hour, even with a squire helping him.

his life competing in a tournament.

Under Attack

It wasn't easy to break into a castle. An attacking army could either try and force its way in, or surround the castle and wait for it to surrender.

▼ A large, wooden catapult, called a trebuchet, was used to sling rocks and stones at a castle's weak points.

siege tower

battering ram

▶ An attacking army fired arrows onto the battlements from a wooden siege tower.

A battering ram was a big, heavy log, used to smash down the door of a castle.

In the 1400s, castles became less

Stones were dropped on an enemy through holes, or machicolations, in the battlement floor.

Weapons included fire, arrows, stones and heavy metal hooks, called grappling irons.

machicolation

important as bigger cannons were made.

Glossary

Chapel
A small church, either within the castle keep or a separate building in the bailey, central to castle life.

Coat-of-arms
A design belonging to a particular person or a group of knights.

Ditcher
A person who dug moats, dungeons, foundations and mines.

Dungeon
An underground prison.

Falcon
A bird of prey that can be trained to hunt for small animals.

Fort
A strong, well-defended building, usually housing soldiers.

Jester
A fool, clown or comedian.

Latrine
A simple kind of toilet, often just a hole in the ground.

Longbow, crossbow
Weapons used for shooting arrows and bolts.

Medieval
A period in history, roughly 600 AD to 1500 AD, also known as the Middle Ages.

Minstrel
A musician or singer.

Pulley
A simple machine used to lift heavy objects.

Quarryman
A workman who dug stone out of a pit in the ground.

Siege engines
Weapons or devices used to try and break down a castle's walls or doors. They included battering rams and large wooden catapults.

Solar
A private room in the castle, lit by large windows.

Squire
A boy training to be a knight.

Stronghold
A well-defended building.

Treadwheel
A huge wooden wheel wide enough for two people to walk inside, side by side. The wheel powered a hoist that lifted heavy stone blocks.

Troubadour
A poet or romantic singer who went from one castle to another and entertained the guests.

Venison
Meat from a deer.

Warlord
A military ruler backed by an army, usually in a country with weak government.